Easy Learning

Design Patterns

Java Practice

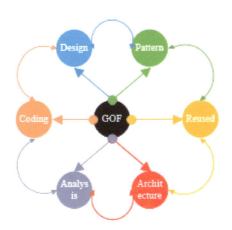

YANG HU

Simple is the beginning of wisdom. From the essence of practice, this book to briefly explain the concept and vividly cultivate programming interest, you will learn it easy and fast.

http://en.verejava.com

ISBN: 9781095899359

CONTENTS

If you want to learn this book, you must have basic knowledge of Java, you can learn book: << Easy Learning Java>>

https://www.amazon.com/dp/1091940339

If you already have basic knowledge of Java, skip it, start an exciting journey

Strategy Pattern Principle

Strategy Pattern: Encapsulates an algorithm inside a class. Define a family of algorithms, encapsulate each one, and make them interchangeable. Strategy lets the algorithm vary independently from clients that use it.

1. Calculate Strategy Addition, subtraction, multiplication, division

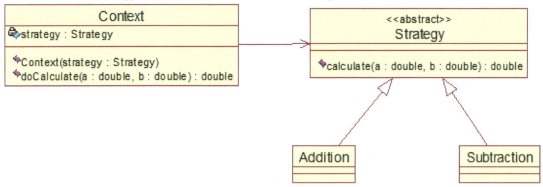

Strategy.java in package com.strategy.principle;

```java
public abstract class Strategy {

    public abstract double calculate(double a,double b);

}
```

Addition.java in package com.strategy.principle;

```java
public class Addition extends Strategy {

    @Override
    public double calculate(double a, double b) {

        return a + b;
    }
}
```

Subtraction.java in package com.strategy.principle;

```java
public class Subtraction extends Strategy {

    @Override
    public double calculate(double a, double b) {

        return a - b;
    }

}
```

Context.java in package com.strategy.principle;

```java
public class Context {
    private Strategy strategy;

    public Context(Strategy strategy) {
        this.strategy = strategy;
    }

    public double doCalculate(double a,double b) {

        return this.strategy.calculate(a, b);
    }
}
```

2. Create a Test class : TestStrategy.java in package com.strategy.principle;

```java
public class TestStrategy {

    public static void main(String[] args) {

        Context ctx = new Context(new Addition());
        double result=ctx.doCalculate(4, 2);
        System.out.println("Addition : "+result);

        ctx = new Context(new Subtraction());
        result=ctx.doCalculate(4, 2);
        System.out.println("Subtraction : "+result);

    }
}
```

Result:

```
Problems   @ Javadoc   Declaration   Console ☒

<terminated> TestStrategy (1) [Java Application] C:\Program Files (x86)\Java\jre6\bin\javaw.exe (2019年
Addition : 6.0
Subtraction : 2.0
```

Strategy Pattern Case

1. Case: E-commerce chooses different banks to pay different strategies

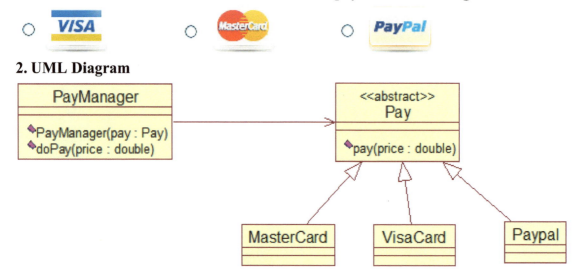

2. UML Diagram

Pay.java in package com.strategy.cases;

```java
public abstract class Pay {

    public abstract void pay(double price);
}
```

MasterCard.java in package com.strategy.cases;

```java
public class MasterCard extends Pay{

    @Override
    public void pay(double price) {

        System.out.println("Pay "+price+" $ by MasterCard");

    }
}
```

VisaCard.java in package com.strategy.cases;

```java
public class VisaCard extends Pay{

    @Override
    public void pay(double price) {

        System.out.println("Pay "+price+" $ by VisaCard");
    }
}
```

Paypal.java in package com.strategy.cases;

```java
public class Paypal extends Pay{

    @Override
    public void pay(double price) {

        System.out.println("Pay "+price+" $ by Paypal");
    }
}
```

PayManager.java in package com.strategy.cases;

```java
public class PayManager {

    private Pay pay;

    public PayManager(Pay pay) {
        this.pay = pay;
    }

    public void doPay(double price) {
        pay.pay(price);
    }

}
```

2. Create a Test class : TestPay.java in package com.strategy.cases;

```java
import java.util.Scanner;
public class TestPay {
    public static void main(String[] args) {

        Scanner in = new Scanner(System.in);
        System.out.println("You need to pay $25  for mobile phone");
        System.out.println("Please select payment method 1: MasterCard 2: VisaCard 3: Paypal");

        int code = in.nextInt();
        PayManager payManager = null;
        if (code == 1) {
            payManager = new PayManager(new MasterCard());
        } else if (code == 2) {
            payManager = new PayManager(new VisaCard());
        } else if (code == 3) {
            payManager = new PayManager(new Paypal());
        }

        payManager.doPay(25);
    }
}
```

Result:

Problems | @ Javadoc | Declaration | Console ☒

<terminated> TestPay (1) [Java Application] C:\Program Files (x86)\Java\jre6\bin\javaw.exe (2019年4月21

```
You need to pay $25  for mobile phone recharge
Please select payment method 1: MasterCard 2: VisaCard 3: Paypal
2
Pay 25.0 $ by VisaCard
```

Composition Pattern Principle

Composition Pattern: A tree structure of simple and composite objects. Compose objects into tree structures to represent part-whole hierarchies. Composite lets clients treat individual objects and compositions of objects uniformly.

1. National city tree diagram

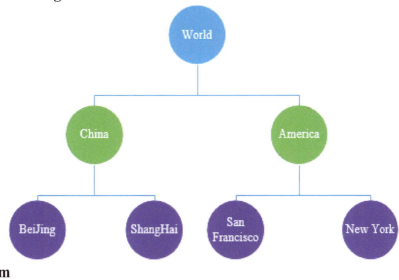

2. UML diagram

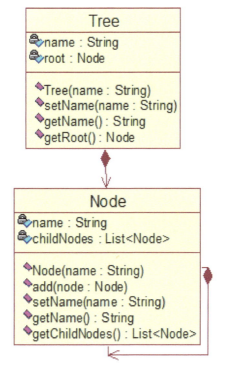

Node.java in package com.composition.principle;

```java
import java.util.*;

public class Node {

    protected String name;
    protected List<Node> childNodes;

    public Node(String name) {
        super();
        this.name = name;
        this.childNodes = new ArrayList<Node>();
    }

    public void add(Node node) {
        childNodes.add(node);
    }

    public String getName() {
        return name;
    }

    public void setName(String name) {
        this.name = name;
    }

    public List<Node> getChildNodes() {
        return childNodes;
    }
}
```

Tree.java in package com.composition.principle;

```java
import java.util.*;

public class Tree {

    private Node root;
    protected String name;

    public Tree(String name) {
        this.root = new Node(name);
    }

    public Node getRoot() {
        return root;
    }

    public String getName() {
        return name;
    }

    public void setName(String name) {
        this.name = name;
    }

}
```

3. Create a Test class : TestTree.java in package com.composition.principle;

```java
import java.util.List;
public class TestTree {
    public static void main(String[] args) {
        Tree tree=new Tree("World");
        Node root = tree.getRoot();

        Node china = new Node("China");
        Node america = new Node("America");
        root.add(china);
        root.add(america);

        Node beijing = new Node("Bei Jing");
        Node shanghai = new Node("Shang Hai");
        china.add(beijing);
        china.add(shanghai);

        Node sanfancisco = new Node("San Fancisco");
        Node newyork = new Node("New York");
        america.add(sanfancisco);
        america.add(newyork);

        System.out.println(root.getName());
        List<Node> childeNodes = root.getChildNodes();
        for (Node node : childeNodes) {
            System.out.println("----" + node.getName());
            List<Node> childNodes2 = node.getChildNodes();
            for (Node node2 : childNodes2) {
                System.out.println("--------" + node2.getName());
            }
        }
    }
}
```

Result:
```
World
----China
--------Bei Jing
--------Shang Hai
----America
--------San Fancisco
--------New York
```

Composition Pattern Case

Java File class is a Composition Pattern.

1. Recursively print all directories and files.

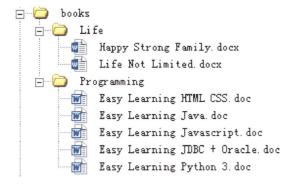

2. UML diagram

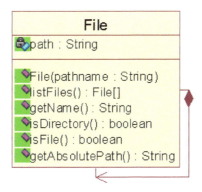

3. Create a Test class : TestFile.java in package com.composition.cases;
Recursively print all directories and files.

```java
import java.io.File;
public class TestFile {
    private static String level = "";

    public static void main(String[] args) {
        showAllDirectory("E:/books");
    }

    public static void showAllDirectory(String path) {
        File dir = new File(path);
        //List all subdirectories and files of the directory
        File[] dirs = dir.listFiles();
        for (int i = 0; dirs != null && i < dirs.length; i++) {
            File f = dirs[i];
            if (f.isFile()) {
                System.out.println(level + f.getName());
            } else if (f.isDirectory()) {
                System.out.println(level + f.getName());
                level += "----";
                showAllDirectory(f.getAbsolutePath());
                level = level.substring(0, level.lastIndexOf("----"));
            }
        }
    }
}
```

Result:

```
Problems  @ Javadoc  Declaration  Console ✕

Life
----Happy Strong Family.docx
----Life Not Limited.docx
Programming
----Easy Learning HTML CSS.doc
----Easy Learning Java.doc
----Easy Learning Javascript.doc
----Easy Learning JDBC + Oracle.doc
----Easy Learning Python 3.doc
```

Singleton Pattern Principle

Singleton Pattern: A class of which only a single instance can exist. Ensure a class only has one instance, and provide a global point of access to it.

1. UML Diagram

Singleton.java in **package com.singleton.principle;**

```java
public class Singleton {

    private static Singleton instance;

    private Singleton() {

    }

    public static Singleton getInstance() {
        if (instance == null) {
            instance = new Singleton(); // there is only one instance
        }
        return instance;
    }
}
```

2. Create a Test class : TestSingleton.java in package com.singleton.principle;

```java
public class TestSingleton {

    public static void main(String[] args) {

        Singleton s1 = Singleton.getInstance();
        Singleton s2 = Singleton.getInstance();

        // the two instances refer to the same address
        System.out.println(s1);
        System.out.println(s2);

    }
}
```

Result:

```
Problems  @ Javadoc  Declaration  Console

<terminated> TestSingleton (1) [Java Application] C:\Program Files (x86)\Java\jre6\bin\javaw.exe (2019年
com.singleton.principle.Singleton@1f1fba0
com.singleton.principle.Singleton@1f1fba0
```

Singleton Pattern Case

Multiple users access a single instance Read config.properties.

1. UML Diagram

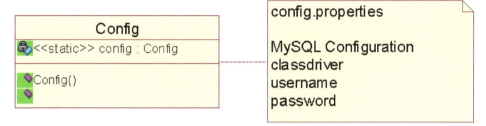

2. The database configuration file config.properties is placed under the Eclipse project src

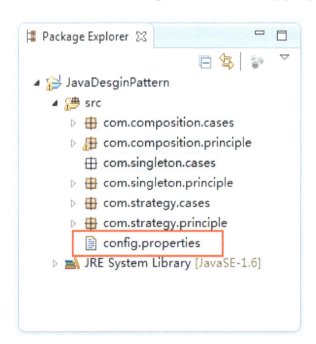

config.properties

```
1 classDriver=jdbc:mysql://localhost/chat?useUnicode=true&characterEncoding=utf-8
2 username=root
3 password=111111
```

Config.java in package com.singleton.cases;

```java
import java.io.*;
import java.util.Properties;

public class Config {
    private static Config config;
    private static Properties p = null;

    public Config() {
        try {
            if (p == null) {
                p = new Properties();
                InputStream is = this.getClass().getResourceAsStream("/config.properties");
                p.load(is); //Load config.properties
            }
        } catch (IOException e) {
            e.printStackTrace();
        }
    }

    public static Config getInstance() {
        if (config == null) {
            config = new Config(); //single instance
        }
        return config;
    }

    //Get the value of with key
    public static String get(String key) {
        return p.getProperty(key);
    }
}
```

3. Create a Test class : TestConfig.java in package com.singleton.cases;

```java
public class TestConfig {

  public static void main(String[] args) {

    Config config1=Config.getInstance();
    System.out.println("Config1 Reference : "+config1);
    System.out.println(config1.get("classDriver"));
    System.out.println(config1.get("username"));
    System.out.println(config1.get("password"));

    System.out.println("-------------------------------------");

    Config config2=Config.getInstance();
    System.out.println("Config2 Reference : "+config2);
    System.out.println(config2.get("classDriver"));
    System.out.println(config2.get("username"));
    System.out.println(config2.get("password"));

  }
}
```

Result:

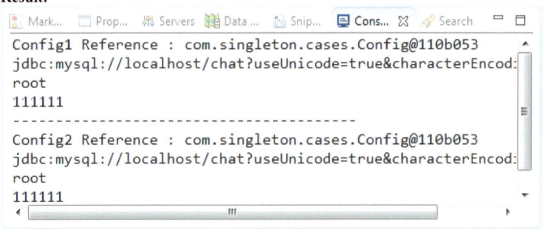

Template Pattern Principle

Template Pattern: Defer the exact steps of an algorithm to a subclass. Define the skeleton of an algorithm in an operation, deferring some steps to subclasses. Template Method lets subclasses redefine certain steps of an algorithm without changing the algorithm's structure.

1. **The parent class prints A4 paper, and the subclass can also set the color.**

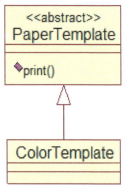

PaperTemplate.java in package com.template.principle;

```java
public abstract class PaperTemplate {

    public void print() {
        System.out.println("Print A4 Paper");
    }
}
```

ColorTemplate.java in package com.template.principle;

```java
public  class ColorTemplate extends PaperTemplate{

    public void print() {
        super.print();

        System.out.println("Set the color of A4 paper red");
    }
}
```

2. Create a Test class : TestTemplate.java in package com.template.principle;

```java
public class TestTemplate {

    public static void main(String[] args) {

        PaperTemplate t = new ColorTemplate();
        t.print();

    }

}
```

Result:

```
Problems  @ Javadoc  Declaration  Console ☒
<terminated> TestTemplate (1) [Java Application] C:\Program Files (x86)\Java\jre6\bin\javaw.e
Print A4 Paper
Set the color of A4 paper red
```

Template Pattern Case

Airplane games:

Different airplane with the same characteristics, but behaves differently

1. UML Diagram

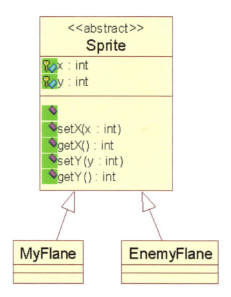

Sprite.java in package com.template.cases;

```java
public abstract class Sprite {

    private int x, y; //Airplane x, y coordinates

    public abstract void draw(); //Draw the plane on the screen

    public int getX() {
        return x;
    }

    public void setX(int x) {
        this.x = x;
    }

    public int getY() {
        return y;
    }

    public void setY(int y) {
        this.y = y;
    }
}
```

MyFlane.java in package com.template.cases;

```java
public class MyFlane extends Sprite {

    @Override
    public void draw() {
        System.out.println("My plane from the bottom of screen : x=" + this.getX() + ",y=" +
this.getY());
    }
}
```

EnemyFlane.java in package com.template.cases;

```java
public class EnemyFlane extends Sprite {

    @Override
    public void draw() {
        System.out.println("Enemy plane from the top of screen : x=" + this.getX() + ",y=" +
this.getY());
    }

}
```

2. Create a Test class : TestSprite.java in package com.template.cases;

```java
public class TestSprite {
    public static void main(String[] args) {
        Sprite mySprite = new MyFlane();
        mySprite.setX(100);
        mySprite.setY(300);
        mySprite.draw();

        Sprite enemySprite = new EnemyFlane();
        enemySprite.setX(0);
        enemySprite.setY(300);
        enemySprite.draw();
    }
}
```

Result:

```
Problems   @ Javadoc   Declaration   Console 

<terminated> TestSprite (1) [Java Application] C:\Program Files (x86)\Java\jre6\bin\javaw.exe
My plane from the bottom of screen : x=100,y=300
Enemy plane from the top of screen : x=0,y=300
```

Factory Pattern Principle

Factory Pattern: Creates an instance of several derived classes. Define an interface for creating an object, but let subclasses decide which class to instantiate. Factory Method lets a class defer instantiation to subclasses.

1. Products can be created by the factory

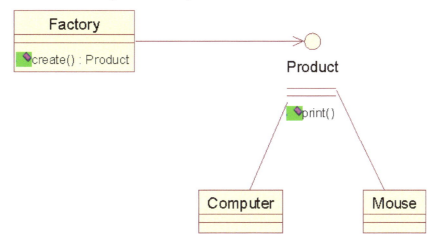

Product.java in **package com.factory.principle;**

```java
public interface Product {

    public void print();
}
```

Computer.java in **package com.factory.principle;**

```java
public class Computer implements Product{

    @Override
    public void print() {
        System.out.println("Dell Computer");
    }
}
```

Mouse.java in package com.factory.principle;

```java
public class Mouse implements Product{

    @Override
    public void print() {
        System.out.println("IBM Mouse");
    }

}
```

Factory.java in package com.factory.principle;

```java
public class Factory {

    public static Product create(int type) {
        Product p = null;
        if (type == 0) //If the type is 0, create Computer
        {
            p = new Computer();
        } else if (type == 1) //If the type is 0, create Mouse
        {
            p = new Mouse();
        }
        return p;
    }
}
```

2. Create a Test class : TestFactory.java in package com.factory.principle;

```java
public class TestFactory {

    public static void main(String[] args) {
        Product p = Factory.create(0);
        p.print();

        p = Factory.create(1);
        p.print();
    }
}
```

Result:

```
Problems  @ Javadoc  Declaration  Console ✕                    ⬜ ☐

                         ■ ✖ ✖ | 📄 🗑 🔲 🔲 | 🔲 🖥 ▾ 🔲 ▾
<terminated> TestFactory (2) [Java Application] C:\Program Files (x86)\Java\jre6\bin\javaw.exe

Dell Computer                                                   ▲
IBM Mouse

                                                               ▼
◀                                                              ▶
```

Factory Pattern Case

Airplane game:

Create different airplane by Factory and then shoot different bullets

1. UML Diagram

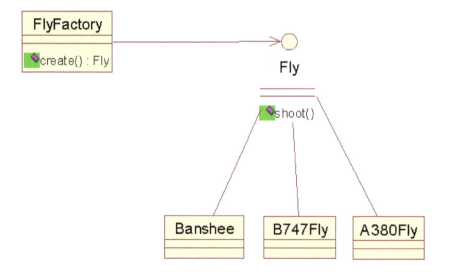

Fly.java in package com.factory.cases;

```java
public interface Fly {

    public void shoot(); //firing bullets

}
```

Banshee.java in package com.factory.cases;

```java
public class Banshee implements Fly {

    @Override
    public void shoot() {
        System.out.println("Banshee fire the laser");
    }

}
```

B747Fly.java in package com.factory.cases;

```java
public class B747Fly implements Fly {

    @Override
    public void shoot() {
        System.out.println("B747 fire the missile");
    }

}
```

A380Fly.java in <inline style="color:orange">package com.factory.cases;</inline>

```java
public class A380Fly implements Fly {

    @Override
    public void shoot() {
        System.out.println("A380 fire the trigeminal shot");
    }

}
```

FlyFactory.java in <inline style="color:orange">package com.factory.cases;</inline>

```java
public class FlyFactory {

    public static Fly create(int type) {

        Fly fly = null;
        if (type == 1) {
            fly = new Banshee();
        } else if (type == 2) {
            fly = new B747Fly();
        } else if (type == 3) {
            fly = new A380Fly();
        }
        return fly;

    }

}
```

2. Create a Test class : TestFactory.java in package com.factory.cases;

```java
import java.util.Scanner;

public class TestFactory {

    public static void main(String[] args) {

        Scanner in = new Scanner(System.in);

        System.out.println("Please select fly 1: Banshee 2: B747 3: A380");

        int type = in.nextInt();

        Fly fly = FlyFactory.create(type);
        fly.shoot();

    }

}
```

Result:

```
Problems  @ Javadoc  Declaration  Console
<terminated> TestFactory (3) [Java Application] C:\Program Files (x86)\Java\jre6\bin\javaw.exe
Please select fly 1: Banshee 2: B747 3: A380
1
Banshee fire the laser
2
B747 fire the missile
3
A380 fire the trigeminal shot
```

Builder Pattern Principle

Builder Pattern: Separates object construction from its representation. Separate the construction of a complex object from its representation so that the same construction processes can create different representations.

1. Car divided into three parts: head, body, wheel.

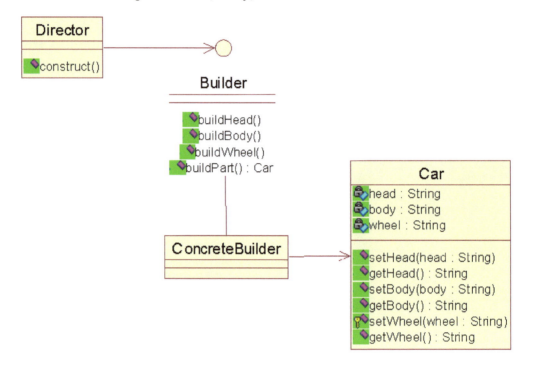

Car.java in package com.builder.principle;

```java
public class Car {
    private String head;
    private String body;
    private String wheel;

    public String getHead() {
        return head;
    }

    public void setHead(String head) {
        this.head = head;
    }

    public String getBody() {
        return body;
    }

    public void setBody(String body) {
        this.body = body;
    }

    public String getWheel() {
        return wheel;
    }

    public void setWheel(String wheel) {
        this.wheel = wheel;
    }
}
```

Builder.java in package com.builder.principle;

```java
public interface Builder {

    public void buildHead();

    public void buildBody();

    public void buildWheel();

    public Car buildPart();
}
```

ConcreteBuilder.java in package com.builder.principle;

```java
public class ConcreteBuilder implements Builder {
    Car car = null;

    public ConcreteBuilder() {
        car = new Car();
    }

    public void buildHead() {
        car.setHead("Car head construction completed");
    }

    public void buildBody() {
        car.setBody("Car body construction completed");
    }

    public void buildWheel() {
        car.setWheel("Car wheel construction completed");
    }

    public Car buildPart() {
        return car;
    }
}
```

Director.java in package com.builder.principle;

```java
public class Director {
    public static Car construct(Builder builder) {

        builder.buildHead();
        builder.buildBody();
        builder.buildWheel();
        return builder.buildPart();

    }
}
```

2. Create a Test class : TestBuilder.java in package com.builder.principle;

```java
public class TestBuilder {

    public static void main(String[] args) {

        Car car = Director.construct(new ConcreteBuilder());
        System.out.println(car.getHead());
        System.out.println(car.getBody());
        System.out.println(car.getWheel());

    }
}
```

Result:

```
Problems  @ Javadoc  Declaration  Console ⌧
<terminated> TestBuilder (1) [Java Application] C:\Program Files (x86)\Java\jre6\bin\javaw.exe
Car head construction completed
Car body construction completed
Car wheel construction completed
```

Builder Pattern Case

Android Dialog:

First create prompts, messages and buttons. And then build dialog to pop up.

1. UML Diagram

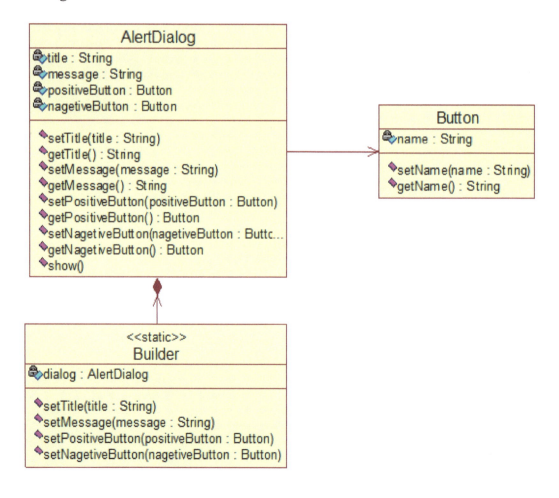

Button.java in package com.builder.cases;

```java
public class Button {
    private String name;

    public Button(String name) {
        super();
        this.name = name;
    }

    public String getName() {
        return name;
    }

    public void setName(String name) {
        this.name = name;
    }
}
```

AlertDialog.java in package com.builder.cases;

```java
public class AlertDialog {
    private String title;
    private String message;
    private Button positiveButton; // Ok button
    private Button nagetiveButton; // Cancel Button

    private AlertDialog() {}

    public String getTitle() {
        return title;
    }

    public void setTitle(String title) {
        this.title = title;
    }

    public String getMessage() {
        return message;
    }

    public void setMessage(String message) {
        this.message = message;
    }

    public Button getPositiveButton() {
        return positiveButton;
    }

    public void setPositiveButton(Button positiveButton) {
        this.positiveButton = positiveButton;
    }

    public Button getNagetiveButton() {
        return nagetiveButton;
    }

    public void setNagetiveButton(Button nagetiveButton) {
        this.nagetiveButton = nagetiveButton;
    }
```

```java
    public void show() {
        System.out.println(this.title);
        System.out.println(this.message);
        System.out.println(this.positiveButton.getName());
        System.out.println(this.nagetiveButton.getName());
        System.out.println("Popup Alert dialog");
    }

    static class Builder {
        private AlertDialog dialog;

        public Builder() {
            dialog = new AlertDialog();
        }

        public void setTitle(String title) {
            dialog.setTitle(title);
        }

        public void setMessage(String message) {
            dialog.setMessage(message);
        }

        public void setPositiveButton(Button positiveButton) {
            dialog.setPositiveButton(positiveButton);
        }

        public void setNagetiveButton(Button nagetiveButton) {
            dialog.setNagetiveButton(nagetiveButton);
        }

        public AlertDialog create() {
            return dialog;
        }
    }
}
```

2. Create a Test class : TestDialog.java in package com.builder.cases;

```java
public class TestDialog {

    public static void main(String[] args) {
        //Build dialog widget
        AlertDialog.Builder builder = new AlertDialog.Builder();
        builder.setTitle("Information");
        builder.setMessage("Confirm exit ?");
        builder.setPositiveButton(new Button("Ok"));
        builder.setNagetiveButton(new Button("Cancel"));

        //Create and pop up a dialog
        AlertDialog dialog = builder.create();
        dialog.show();
    }

}
```

Result:

```
Problems  @ Javadoc  Declaration  Console ⌗

<terminated> TestDialog (1) [Java Application] C:\Program Files (x86)\Java\jre6\bin\javaw.exe
Information
Confirm exit ?
Ok
Cancel
Popup Alert dialog
```

Adapter Pattern Principle

Adapter Pattern: Match interfaces of different classes.Convert the interface of a class into another interface clients expect. Adapter lets classes work together that couldn't otherwise because of incompatible interfaces.

1. **The original power is 100 voltages, and it needs to be adapted to 36 voltages.**

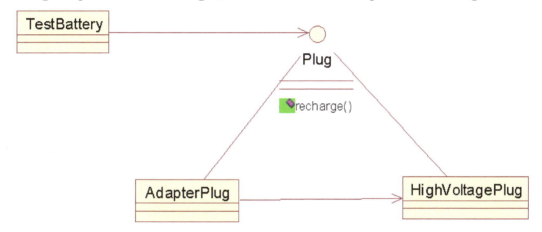

Plug.java in **package com.adapter.principle;**

```java
public interface Plug {

    public int recharge();
}
```

HighVoltagePlug.java in **package com.adapter.principle;**

```java
public class HighVoltagePlug implements Plug {

    public int recharge() {
        return 100; //Power is 100 Voltage
    }

}
```

AdapterPlug.java in **package com.adapter.principle;**

```java
public class AdapterPlug implements Plug {

    @Override
    public int recharge() {
        HighVoltagePlug bigplug = new HighVoltagePlug();
        int v = bigplug.recharge();
        v = v - 64;
        return v;
    }
}
```

2. Create a Test class : **TestBattery.java in package com.adapter.principle;**

```java
public class TestBattery {

    public static void main(String[] args) {
        Plug plug = new HighVoltagePlug();
        System.out.println(plug.recharge() + " too much voltage");

        plug = new AdapterPlug();
        System.out.println("Adapter into " + plug.recharge() + " voltage");
    }
}
```

Result:

```
Problems  @ Javadoc  Declaration  Console

<terminated> TestBattery (1) [Java Application] C:\Program Files (x86)\Java\jre6\bin\javaw.exe
100 too much voltage
Adapter into 36 voltage
```

Adapter Pattern Case

Android ListView:

ListView data is filled, the same data but different adaptor show different view

1. UML Diagram

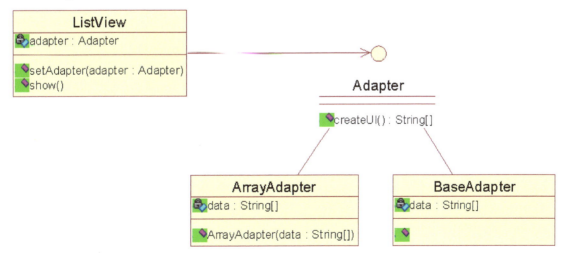

Adapter.java in package com.adapter.cases;

```java
public interface Adapter {

    public String[] createUI(); //Creating UI display data

}
```

ArrayAdapter.java in package com.adapter.cases;

```java
public class ArrayAdapter implements Adapter {

    private String[] data;

    public ArrayAdapter(String[] data) {
        this.data = data;
    }

    @Override
    public String[] createUI() {
        return this.data;
    }
}
```

BaseAdapter.java in package com.adapter.cases;

```java
//adapter for images
public class BaseAdapter implements Adapter {

    private String[] data;

    public BaseAdapter(String[] data) {
        this.data = data;
    }

    @Override
    public String[] createUI() {
        for (int i = 0; i < data.length; i++) {
            data[i] = "Image : " + data[i];
        }
        return this.data;
    }
}
```

ListView.java in package com.adapter.cases;

```java
public class ListView {

    private Adapter adapter;

    public void setAdapter(Adapter adapter) {
        this.adapter = adapter;
    }

    public void show() {
        String[] data = adapter.createUI();
        for (String str : data) {
            System.out.println(str);
        }
    }
}
```

2. Create a Test class : TestAdapter.java in package com.adapter.cases;

```java
public class TestAdapter {

    public static void main(String[] args) {
        String[] data = {
                            "Happy Strong Family",
                            "Easy Learning Java",
                            "Easy Learning Python 3",
                            "Easy Learing HTML CSS",
                            "Easy Learning Javascript"
                        };
        ListView listView = new ListView();
        listView.setAdapter(new ArrayAdapter(data));
        listView.show();

        System.out.println("-------------------------------------");

        listView.setAdapter(new BaseAdapter(data));
        listView.show();
    }
}
```

Result:

```
Problems  @ Javadoc  Declaration  Console

<terminated> TestAdapter (1) [Java Application] C:\Program Files (x86)\Java\jre6\bin\javaw.e>
Happy Strong Family
Easy Learning Java
Easy Learning Python 3
Easy Learing HTML CSS
Easy Learning Javascript
-------------------------------------
Image : Happy Strong Family
Image : Easy Learning Java
Image : Easy Learning Python 3
Image : Easy Learing HTML CSS
Image : Easy Learning Javascript
```

Facade Pattern Principle

Facade Pattern: A single class that represents an entire subsystem. Provide a unified interface to a set of interfaces in a system. Facade defines a higher-level interface that makes the subsystem easier to use.

1. State provide a consistent interface to perform :
Light, music and video.

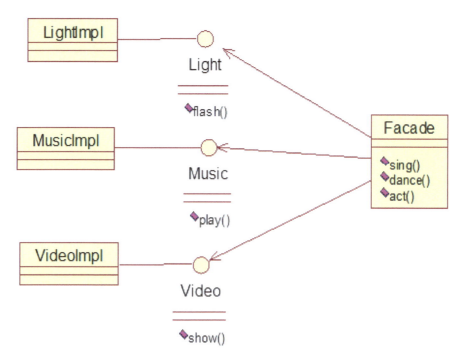

Light.java in **package com.facade.principle;**

```java
public interface Light {
    public void flash();
}
```

LightImpl.java in **package com.facade.principle;**

```java
public class LightImpl implements Light {
    public void flash() {
    System.out.println("Flashing color light");
    }
}
```

Music.java in package com.facade.principle;

```java
public interface Music {

    public void play();
}
```

MusicImpl.java in package com.facade.principle;

```java
public class MusicImpl implements Music {

    @Override
    public void play() {
        System.out.println("Playing classical music");
    }
}
```

Video.java in package com.facade.principle;

```java
public interface Video {

    public void show();
}
```

VideoImpl.java in package com.facade.principle;

```java
public class VideoImpl implements Video {

    @Override
    public void show() {
        System.out.println("Mountain stream video display");
    }
}
```

Facade.java in **package com.facade.principle;**

```java
//provides a consistent interface to call
public class Facade {

    private Light light;
    private Music music;
    private Video video;

    public Facade() {
        light = new LightImpl();
        music = new MusicImpl();
        video = new VideoImpl();
    }

    public void sing() {
        System.out.println("Start singing with ");
        light.flash();
        music.play();
    }

    public void dance() {
        System.out.println("Start dancing with ");
        light.flash();
        music.play();
        video.show();
    }

    public void act() {
        System.out.println("Start acting with ");
        light.flash();
        video.show();
    }
}
```

2. Create a Test class : TestFacade.java in package com.facade.principle;

```java
public class TestFacade {

    public static void main(String[] args) {
        Facade facade = new Facade();

        facade.sing();

        System.out.println("-----------------------------");

        facade.dance();

        System.out.println("-----------------------------");

        facade.act();
    }
}
```

Result:

```
Problems  @ Javadoc  Declaration  Console

<terminated> TestFacade (1) [Java Application] C:\Program Files (x86)\Java\jre6\bin\javaw.exe
Start singing with
Flashing color light
Playing classical music
-----------------------------
Start dancing with
Flashing color light
Playing classical music
Mountain stream video display
-----------------------------
Start acting with
Flashing color light
Mountain stream video display
```

Facade Pattern Case

1. JDBC into DBUtil class that provide consistent interface to call

If you want to learn JDBC + MySQL or Oracle please read book

<<Easy Learning JDBC + MySQL>> <<Easy Learning JDBC + Oracle>>

http://en.verejava.com

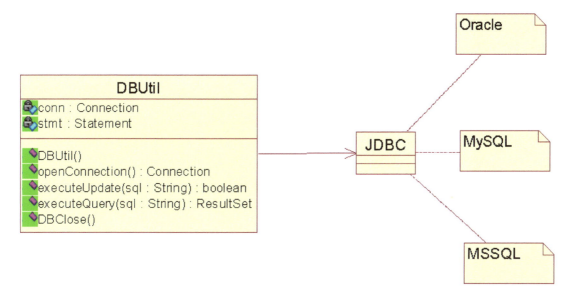

DBUtil.java in **package com.facade.cases;**

```
import java.sql.*;
import java.util.Date;
public class DBUtil {
   protected Connection conn;
   protected Statement stmt;

   public DBUtil() {
      try {
         Class.forName("com.mysql.jdbc.Driver");
      } catch (ClassNotFoundException e) {
         e.printStackTrace();
      }
   }
}
```

```java
    public Connection openConnection() {
        try {
            return
DriverManager.getConnection("jdbc:mysql://localhost/test?useUnicode=true&characterEncod
ing=utf-8", "root", "19810109");
        } catch (SQLException e) {
            e.printStackTrace();
        }
        return null;
    }

    public boolean executeUpdate(String sql) {
        conn = openConnection();

        try {
            Statement stmt = conn.createStatement();
            if (stmt.executeUpdate(sql) > 0) {
                return true;
            }
        } catch (SQLException e) {
            e.printStackTrace();
        } finally {
            if (conn != null) {
                try {
                    conn.close();
                } catch (SQLException e) {
                    e.printStackTrace();
                }
            }
        }
        return false;
    }

    public ResultSet executeQuery(String sql) {
        conn = openConnection();
        try {
            Statement stmt = conn.createStatement();
            return stmt.executeQuery(sql);
        } catch (SQLException e) {
            e.printStackTrace();
        }
        return null;
    }
}
```

```java
public void DBClose() {
    if (conn != null) {
        try {
            conn.close();
        } catch (SQLException e) {
            e.printStackTrace();
        }
    }
}
```

TestDBUtil.java in package com.facade.cases;

```java
import java.sql.ResultSet;
import java.sql.SQLException;

public class TestDBUtil {

  public static void main(String[] args) {
    //Add User
    DBUtil db = new DBUtil();
    String sql = "insert into users(username,pwd)values('david','444444')";
    db.executeUpdate(sql);

    //Update User
    sql = "update users set pwd='555555' where id=3";
    db.executeUpdate(sql);

    //Query from User
    sql = "select * from users";
    ResultSet rs = db.executeQuery(sql);
    try {
      while (rs.ncxt()) {
        int id = rs.getInt("id");
        String username = rs.getString("username");
        String pwd = rs.getString("pwd");
        System.out.println(id + "," + username + "," + pwd);
      }
    } catch (SQLException e) {
      e.printStackTrace();
    } finally {
      db.DBClose();
    }

    //Delete User
    sql = "delete from users where id=3";
    db.executeUpdate(sql);
  }
}
```

Decorator Pattern Principle

Decorator Pattern: Add responsibilities to objects dynamically. Attach additional responsibilities to an object dynamically. Decorators provide a flexible alternative to subclassing for extending functionality.

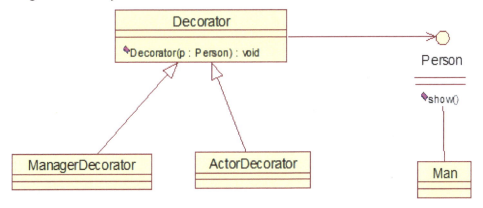

Person.java in **package com.decorator.principle;**

```java
public interface Person {
    public void show();
}
```

Man.java in **package com.decorator.principle;**

```java
public class Man implements Person {
    public void show() {
        System.out.println("I am a man");
    }
}
```

Decorator.java in **package com.decorator.principle;**

```java
public abstract class Decorator implements Person {
    protected Person p;

    public Decorator(Person p) {
        this.p = p;
    }
}
```

ManagerDecorator.java in package com.decorator.principle;

```java
public class ManagerDecorator extends Decorator {

    public ManagerDecorator(Person p) {
        super(p);
    }

    @Override
    public void show() {
        p.show();
        System.out.println("I am still a manager");
    }

}
```

ActorDecorator.java in package com.decorator.principle;

```java
public class ActorDecorator extends Decorator {

    public ActorDecorator(Person p) {
        super(p);
    }

    @Override
    public void show() {
        p.show();
        System.out.println("I am still an international actor.");
    }

}
```

2. Create a Test class : TestDecorator.java in package com.decorator.principle;

```java
public class TestDecorator {

    public static void main(String[] args) {

        Person p = new Man();
        p.show();

        p = new ManagerDecorator(p);
        p.show();

        p = new ActorDecorator(p);
        p.show();

    }

}
```

Result:

```
Problems  @ Javadoc  Declaration  Console ✕

<terminated> TestDecorator (1) [Java Application] C:\Program Files (x86)\Java\jre6\bin\javaw.
I am a man
----------------------------
I am a man
I am still a manager
----------------------------
I am a man
I am still a manager
I am still an international actor.
```

Decorator Pattern Case

The Java IO is a decorator pattern.
The same data file can be decorated as a InputStream, or as a FileReader. etc.

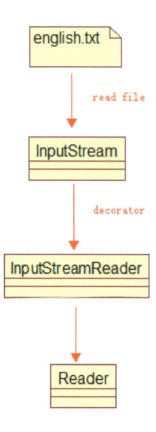

2. Create a Test class : TestIO.java in package com.decorator.cases;

```java
import java.io.*;

public class TestIO {

  public static void main(String[] args) {
    InputStream is = null;
    try {
      //Decorate file data into a FileInputStream
      is = new FileInputStream("english.txt");

      //The byte stream can be re-decorated into a Reader
      Reader reader = new InputStreamReader(is);
      int l;
      while ((l = reader.read()) != -1) {
        System.out.println((char) l);
      }
    } catch (Exception e) {
      e.printStackTrace();
    } finally {
      try {
        is.close();
      } catch (IOException e) {
        e.printStackTrace();
      }
    }
  }
}
```

Prototype Pattern Shallow Clone

Prototype Pattern :
Specify the kinds of objects you create, and create new ones by copying them.

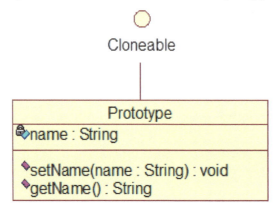

Shallow clones only copy basic data types

Prototype.java in package com.clone.shallow;

```java
public class Prototype implements Cloneable {
    private String name;

    public Prototype(String name) {
        super();
        this.name = name;
    }

    public String getName() {
        return name;
    }

    public void setName(String name) {
        this.name = name;
    }

    @Override
    protected Object clone() {
        Prototype p = null;
        try {
            p = (Prototype) super.clone();
        } catch (CloneNotSupportedException e) {
            e.printStackTrace();
        }
        return p;
    }

}
```

1. Create a Test class : TestClone.java in package com.clone.shallow;

```java
public class TestClone {

    public static void main(String[] args) {

        Prototype p = new Prototype("David");
        System.out.println(p.getName());

        System.out.println("-------------------");

        Prototype p2 = (Prototype) p.clone();
        System.out.println(p2.getName());

    }

}
```

Result:

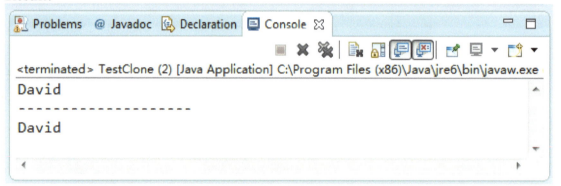

Prototype Pattern Deep Clone

Prototype Pattern :
Specify the kinds of objects you create, and create new ones by copying them.

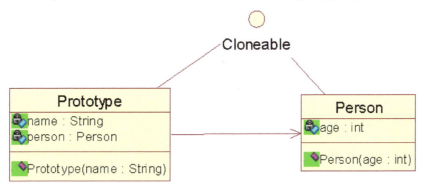

Deep clones can copy object.

Person.java in

```java
public class Person implements Cloneable {
   private int age;

   public Person(int age) {
      super();
      this.age = age;
   }

   public int getAge() {
      return age;
   }

   public void setAge(int age) {
      this.age = age;
   }

   @Override
   protected Object clone() {

      try {
         return super.clone();
      } catch (CloneNotSupportedException e) {
         e.printStackTrace();
      }
      return null;
   }

}
```

Prototype.java in package com.clone.shallow;

```java
public class Prototype implements Cloneable {
    private String name;
    private Person person;

    public Prototype(String name) {
        super();
        this.name = name;
    }

    public String getName() {
        return name;
    }

    public void setName(String name) {
        this.name = name;
    }

    public Person getPerson() {
        return person;
    }

    public void setPerson(Person person) {
        this.person = person;
    }

    protected Object clone() {
        Prototype p = null;
        try {
            p = (Prototype) super.clone();

            if (person != null) {
                Object obj = person.clone();
                p.person = (Person) obj;
            }
        } catch (CloneNotSupportedException e) {
            e.printStackTrace();
        }
        return p;
    }
}
```

1. Create a Test class : TestDeepClone.java in package com.clone.shallow;

```java
public class TestDeepClone {

    public static void main(String[] args) {

        Prototype p = new Prototype("David");
        p.setPerson(new Person(20));
        System.out.println(p.getName() + "," + p.getPerson().getAge());

        System.out.println("-------------------------");

        Prototype p2 = (Prototype) p.clone();
        System.out.println(p2.getName() + "," + p.getPerson().getAge());

    }

}
```

Result:

```
Problems   @ Javadoc   Declaration   Console

<terminated> TestDeepClone (1) [Java Application] C:\Program Files (x86)\Java\jre6\bin\javaw
David,20
-------------------------
David,20
```

Bridge Pattern Principle

Bridge Pattern : Separates an object's interface from its implementation. Decouple an abstraction from its implementation so that the two can vary independently.

1. Different people can wear different clothes

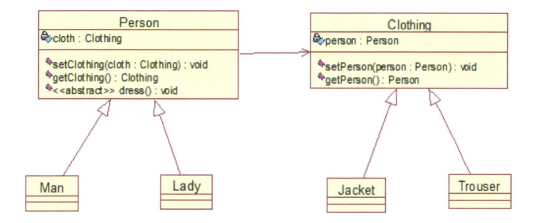

Person.java in package com.bridge.principle;

```java
public abstract class Person {

    protected String name;
    protected Clothing cloth;

    public Person(String name) {
        super();
        this.name = name;
    }

    public String getName() {
        return name;
    }

    public void setName(String name) {
        this.name = name;
    }

    public Clothing getCloth() {
        return cloth;
    }

    public void setCloth(Clothing cloth) {
        this.cloth = cloth;
    }

    public abstract void dress();
}
```

Man.java in package com.bridge.principle;

```java
public class Man extends Person {

    public Man(String name) {
        super(name);
    }

    @Override
    public void dress() {
        System.out.println(name + " wear " + cloth.getName());
    }

}
```

Lady.java in package com.bridge.principle;

```java
public class Lady extends Person {

    public Lady(String name) {
        super(name);
    }

    @Override
    public void dress() {
        System.out.println(name + " wear " + cloth.getName());
    }

}
```

Clothing.java in package com.bridge.principle;

```java
public abstract class Clothing {

    protected String name;
    protected Person person;

    public Clothing(String name) {
        super();
        this.name = name;
    }

    public String getName() {
        return name;
    }

    public void setName(String name) {
        this.name = name;
    }

    public Person getPerson() {
        return person;
    }

    public void setPerson(Person person) {
        this.person = person;
    }
}
```

Jacket.java in

```java
public class Jacket extends Clothing {

    public Jacket(String name) {
        super(name);
    }

}
```

Trouser.java in

```java
public class Trouser extends Clothing {

    public Trouser(String name) {
        super(name);
    }

}
```

2. Create a Test class : TestBrige.java in package com.bridge.principle;

```java
public class TestBrige {

    public static void main(String[] args) {

        Person man = new Man("Man");
        Person lady = new Lady("Lady");

        Clothing jacket = new Jacket("Jacket");
        Clothing trouser = new Trouser("Trouser");

        man.setCloth(jacket); //Man wear Jacket
        man.dress();

        man.setCloth(trouser); //Man wear Trouser
        man.dress();

        lady.setCloth(jacket); //Lady wear Jacket
        lady.dress();

        lady.setCloth(trouscr); //Lady wear Trouser
        lady.dress();
    }

}
```

Result:

```
Problems  @ Javadoc  Declaration  Console

<terminated> TestBrige (1) [Java Application] C:\Program Files (x86)\Java\jre6\bin\javaw.exe (

Man wear Jacket
Man wear Trouser
Lady wear Jacket
Lady wear Trouser
```

Bridge Pattern Case

Bridge Pattern :
Separate the abstract from implementation so that they can all change independently.

1. Different airplane fire different bullets

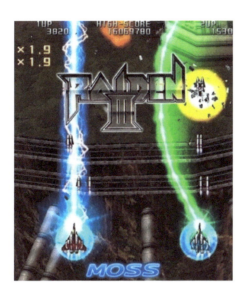

2. UML Diagram

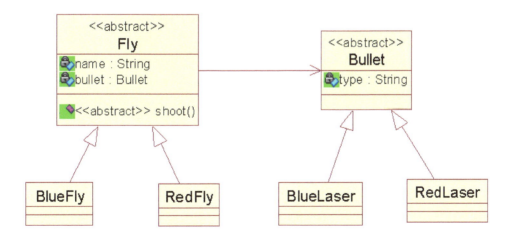

Bullet.java in

```java
public abstract class Bullet {

    protected String type;

    public Bullet(String type) {
        super();
        this.type = type;
    }

    public String getType() {
        return type;
    }

    public void setType(String type) {
        this.type = type;
    }
}
```

BlueLaser.java in package com.bridge.cases;

```java
public class BlueLaser extends Bullet {

    public BlueLaser(String type) {
        super(type);
    }
}
```

RedLaser.java in package com.bridge.cases;

```java
public class RedLaser extends Bullet {

    public RedLaser(String type) {
        super(type);
    }
}
```

Fly.java in package com.bridge.cases;

```java
public abstract class Fly {
    protected String name;
    protected Bullet bullet;

    public Fly(String name) {
        super();
        this.name = name;
    }

    public abstract void shoot();

    public String getName() {
        return name;
    }

    public void setName(String name) {
        this.name = name;
    }

    public Bullet getBullet() {
        return bullet;
    }

    public void setBullet(Bullet bullet) {
        this.bullet = bullet;
    }
}
```

BlueFly.java in package com.bridge.cases;

```java
public class BlueFly extends Fly {
    public BlueFly(String name) {
        super(name);
    }

    @Override
    public void shoot() {
        System.out.println(name + " fire " + bullet.getType());
    }
}
```

RedFly.java in package com.bridge.cases;

```java
public class RedFly extends Fly {
    public RedFly(String name) {
        super(name);
    }

    @Override
    public void shoot() {
        System.out.println(name + " fire " + bullet.getType());
    }
}
```

2. Create a Test class : TestFly.java in package com.bridge.cases;

```java
public class TestFly {
    public static void main(String[] args) {
        Fly blueFly = new BlueFly("BlueFly");
        Fly redFly = new RedFly("RedFly");

        Bullet blueLaser = new BlueLaser("BlueLaser");
        Bullet redLaser = new RedLaser("RedLaser");

        blueFly.setBullet(blueLaser);//BlueFly fire BlueLaser
        blueFly.shoot();

        blueFly.setBullet(redLaser);//BlueFly fire RedLaser
        blueFly.shoot();

        redFly.setBullet(blueLaser);//RedFly fire BlueLaser
        redFly.shoot();

        redFly.setBullet(redLaser);//RedFly fire RedLaser
        redFly.shoot();
    }
}
```

Result:

```
Problems  @ Javadoc  Declaration  Console

<terminated> TestFly (1) [Java Application] C:\Program Files (x86)\Java\jre6\bin\javaw.exe (20

BlueFly fire BlueLaser
BlueFly fire RedLaser
RedFly fire BlueLaser
RedFly fire RedLaser
```

FlyWeight Pattern Case

FlyWeight Pattern : A fine-grained instance used for efficient sharing. Use sharing to support large numbers of fine-grained objects efficiently. A flyweight is a shared object that can be used in multiple contexts simultaneously. The flyweight acts as an independent object in each context — it's indistinguishable from an instance of the object that's not shared.

Some data can be stored in the cache. The client can get the data directly from the cache and improve the speed.

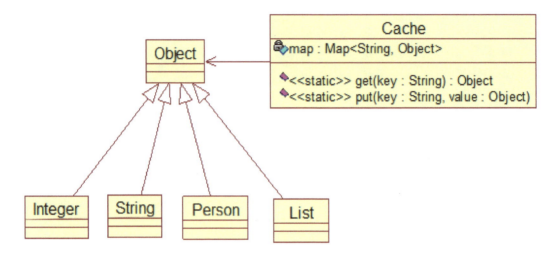

Cache.java in package com.flyweight.cases;

```java
import java.util.*;
public class Cache {
    private static Map<String, Object> map = new HashMap<String, Object>();

    public static Object get(String key) {
        return map.get(key);
    }

    public static void put(String key, Object value) {
        map.put(key, value);
    }

    public static void remove(String key) {
        map.remove(key);
    }
}
```

Person.java in package com.flyweight.cases;

```java
public class Person {
    private String name;

    public Person() {
    }

    public Person(String name) {
        this.name = name;
    }

    public String getName() {
        return name;
    }

    public void setName(String name) {
        this.name = name;
    }
}
```

2. Create a Test class : TestCache.java in package com.flyweight.cases;

```java
import java.util.*;

public class TestCache {

    public static void main(String[] args) {
        //Basic data types are stored in the cache
        Cache.put("1", 1000);

        //String are stored in the cache
        Cache.put("name", "Grace");

        //Object are stored in the cache
        Cache.put("person", new Person("Sala"));

        //Get data from the cache
        System.out.println(Cache.get("1"));

        System.out.println(Cache.get("name"));

        Person p = (Person) Cache.get("person");
        System.out.println(p.getName());
    }
}
```

Result:

```
Problems  @ Javadoc  Declaration  Console ⊠

<terminated> TestCache (1) [Java Application] C:\Program Files (x86)\Java\jre6\bin\javaw.exe
1000
Grace
Sala
```

Chain Pattern Principle

Chain Pattern : A way of passing a request between a chain of objects. Avoid coupling the sender of a request to its receiver by giving more than one object a chance to handle the request. Chain the receiving objects and pass the request along the chain until an object handles it.

1. Resignation Apply -> Financial Review -> Manager Review -> Approval

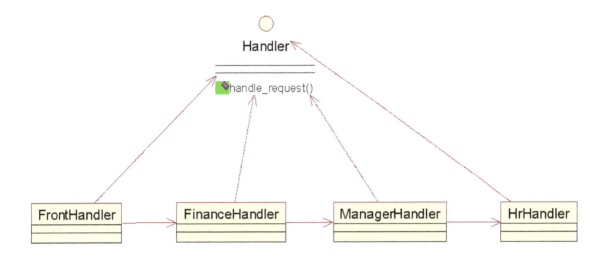

Handler.java in package com.chain.principle;

```java
public interface Handler {

    public void handleRequest(String request);

}
```

FrontHandler.java in package com.chain.principle;

```java
public class FrontHandler implements Handler {
  private Handler nextHandler;

  public FrontHandler(Handler nextHandler) {
    this.nextHandler = nextHandler;
  }

  @Override
  public void handleRequest(String request) {
    if ("ResignationApply".equals(request)) {
      System.out.println("Resignation Apply");
      if (nextHandler != null)
        nextHandler.handleRequest("FinancialReview");
    }
  }
}
```

FinanceHandler.java in package com.chain.principle;

```java
public class FinanceHandler implements Handler {
  private Handler nextHandler;

  public FinanceHandler(Handler nextHandler) {
    this.nextHandler = nextHandler;
  }

  @Override
  public void handleRequest(String request) {
    if ("FinancialReview".equals(request)) {
      System.out.println("Financial Review Completed");
      if (nextHandler != null)
        nextHandler.handleRequest("ManagerReview");
    }
  }
}
```

ManagerHandler.java in package com.chain.principle;

```java
public class ManagerHandler implements Handler {
    private Handler nextHandler;

    public ManagerHandler(Handler nextHandler) {
        this.nextHandler = nextHandler;
    }

    @Override
    public void handleRequest(String request) {
        if ("ManagerReview".equals(request)) {
            System.out.println("Manager Review Completed");
            if (nextHandler != null)
                nextHandler.handleRequest("Approval");
        }
    }
}
```

HrHandler.java in package com.chain.principle;

```java
public class HrHandler implements Handler {
    private Handler nextHandler;

    public HrHandler (Handler nextHandler) {
        this.nextHandler = nextHandler;
    }

    @Override
    public void handleRequest(String request) {
        if ("Approval".equals(request)) {
            System.out.println("HR Approval");
            if (nextHandler != null)
                nextHandler.handleRequest("Approval Completed");
        }
    }
}
```

2. Create a Test class : TestHandler.java **in** package com.chain.principle;

```java
public class TestHandler {

  public static void main(String[] args) {

    Handler hrHandler = new HrHandler(null);
    Handler managerHandler = new ManagerHandler(hrHandler);
    Handler financeHandler = new FinanceHandler(managerHandler);
    Handler frontHandler = new FrontHandler(financeHandler);

    frontHandler.handleRequest("ResignationApply");
  }
}
```

Result:

```
Problems  @ Javadoc  Declaration  Console ⌗                                  ⬜ ⬛

                              ⬛ ✖ ✖ | ▤ ▦ ▣ ▣ | ✎ ⬛ ▾ ⬜ ▾
<terminated> TestHandler (1) [Java Application] C:\Program Files (x86)\Java\jre6\bin\javaw.ex
Resignation Apply                                                              ▲
Financial Review Completed
Manager Review Completed
HR Approval


                                                                               ▼
◄                                                                          ►
```

Chain Pattern Case

Chain Pattern :
Give multiple objects to process the request in chain.

1. Java Web Filter or VereMVC Web Framework Interceptor

http://en.verejava.com/?section_id=1697715673191

2. Authority Authentication -> Set Character -> Business Preprocessing

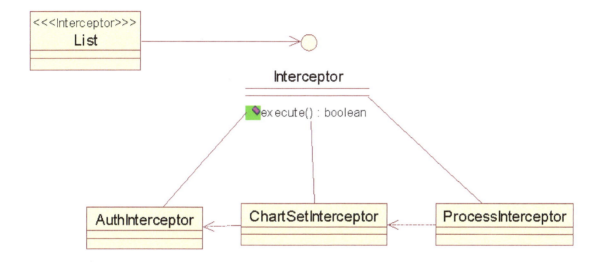

Interceptor.java in package com.chain.cases;

```
public interface Interceptor {

    public boolean execute();

}
```

AuthInterceptor.java in package com.chain.cases;

```java
public class AuthInterceptor implements Interceptor {

  @Override
  public boolean execute() {
    System.out.println("Authority Authentication");
    return true;
  }

}
```

ChartSetInterceptor.java in package com.chain.cases;

```java
public class ChartSetInterceptor implements Interceptor {

  @Override
  public boolean execute() {
    System.out.println("Set Character");
    return true;
  }

}
```

ProcessInterceptor.java in package com.chain.cases;

```java
public class ProcessInterceptor implements Interceptor {

  @Override
  public boolean execute() {
    System.out.println("Business Preprocessing");
    return true;
  }

}
```

3. Create a Test class : TestIntercepter.java in package com.chain.cases;

```java
import java.util.*;

public class TestIntercepter {

    public static void main(String[] args) {

        List<Interceptor> interceptorList = new ArrayList<Interceptor>();
        interceptorList.add(new AuthInterceptor());
        interceptorList.add(new ChartSetInterceptor());
        interceptorList.add(new ProcessInterceptor());

        for (int i = 0; i < interceptorList.size(); i++) {
            Interceptor interceptor = interceptorList.get(i);
            boolean isNextInvoke = interceptor.execute();

            if (!isNextInvoke) {
                break;
            }
        }
    }
}
```

Result:

```
Problems  @ Javadoc  Declaration  Console

<terminated> TestIntercepter (1) [Java Application] C:\Program Files (x86)\Java\jre6\bin\javaw

Authority Authentication
Set Character
Business Preprocessing
```

Command Pattern Case

Command Pattern :
Encapsulate a request as an object, allowing you to parameterize different requests.

1. Button event, mouse click Ok or Cancel Button.

2. UML Diagram

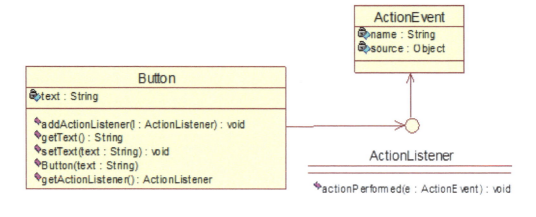

ActionListener.java in package com.command.cases;

```java
public interface ActionListener {

    public void actionPerformed(ActionEvent e);

}
```

ActionEvent.java in package com.command.cases;

```java
public class ActionEvent {
    private String name;
    private Object source;

    public ActionEvent(String name, Object source) {
        super();
        this.name = name;
        this.source = source;
    }

    public String getName() {
        return name;
    }

    public void setName(String name) {
        this.name = name;
    }

    public Object getSource() {
        return source;
    }

    public void setSource(Object source) {
        this.source = source;
    }
}
```

Button.java in package com.command.cases;

```java
public class Button {
   private ActionListener actionListener;
   private String text;

   public Button(String text) {
      super();
      this.text = text;
   }

   public ActionListener getActionListener() {
      return actionListener;
   }

   public void addActionListener(ActionListener actionListener) {
      this.actionListener = actionListener;
   }

   public String getText() {
      return text;
   }

   public void setText(String text) {
      this.text = text;
   }
}
```

Mouse.java in package com.command.cases;

```java
public class Mouse {

   public void click(Button btn) {
      ActionEvent e = new ActionEvent(btn.getText(), btn);
      btn.getActionListener().actionPerformed(e);
   }

}
```

3. Create a Test class : TestCommand.java in package com.command.cases;

```java
import java.util.ArrayList;
public class TestCommand {

    public static void main(String[] args) {
        Button btnOk = new Button("Ok");
        Button btnCancel = new Button("Cancel");

        btnOk.addActionListener(new ActionListener() { //Add a listen event
            @Override
            public void actionPerformed(ActionEvent e) {
                System.out.println("OK button is clicked");
            }
        });

        btnCancel.addActionListener(new ActionListener() {//Add a listen event
            @Override
            public void actionPerformed(ActionEvent e) {
                System.out.println("Cancel button is clicked");
            }
        });

        Mouse m = new Mouse();
        m.click(btnOk); //Mouse click OK button
        m.click(btnCancel);//Mouse click Cancel button
    }
}
```

Result:

Problems @ Javadoc Declaration Console ⊠

`<terminated> TestCommand (1) [Java Application] C:\Program Files (x86)\Java\jre6\bin\javaw`

```
OK button is clicked
Cancel button is clicked
```

Iterator Pattern Case

Iterator Pattern : Sequentially access the elements of a collection. Provide a way to access the elements of an aggregate object sequentially without exposing its underlying representation.

1. Implement the iterator in Javascript

2. UML Diagram

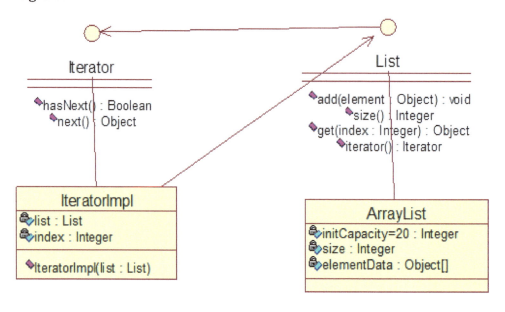

Iterator.java in package com.iterator.cases;

```java
public interface Iterator {

    public boolean hasNext();

    public Object next();

}
```

IteratorImpl.java in package com.iterator.cases;

```java
public class IteratorImpl implements Iterator {
    private int index;
    private List list;

    public IteratorImpl(List list) {
        this.list = list;
    }

    @Override
    public boolean hasNext() {
        return index < list.size();
    }

    @Override
    public Object next() {
        Object element = null;
        if (index < list.size()) {
            element = list.get(index);
            index++;
        }
        return element;
    }

}
```

List.java in package com.iterator.cases;

```java
public interface List {

    public void add(Object element);

    public Object get(int index);

    public int size();

    public Iterator iterator();

}
```

ArrayList.java in **package com.iterator.cases;**

```java
import java.util.Arrays;

public class ArrayList implements List {
    private int initCapacit = 20;
    private int size;
    private Object[] elementData;

    public ArrayList() {
        elementData = new Object[initCapacit];
    }

    @Override
    public void add(Object element) {
        if (size < initCapacit) {
            elementData[size] = element;
            size++;
        } else {
            elementData = Arrays.copyOf(elementData, size);
            elementData[size] = element;
            size++;
        }
    }

    @Override
    public Object get(int index) {
        return elementData[index];
    }

    @Override
    public int size() {
        return size;
    }

    @Override
    public Iterator iterator() {
        return new IteratorImpl(this);
    }
}
```

3. Create a Test class : TestIterator.java in package com.iterator.cases;

```java
public class TestIterator {

    public static void main(String[] args) {
        List list = new ArrayList();
        list.add("Berkeley University");
        list.add("Market Street");
        list.add("Polo Alto");
        list.add("Cuptino");

        Iterator iter = list.iterator();
        while (iter.hasNext()) {
            Object obj = iter.next();
            System.out.println(obj);
        }
    }

}
```

Result:

```
Problems   @ Javadoc   Declaration   Console ⋈                          ▭ ▢

                              ■ ✖ ✖ | ⬛ ⬛ ⬛ ⬛ | ⬛ ⬛ ▾ ⬛ ▾
<terminated> TestIterator (3) [Java Application] C:\Program Files (x86)\Java\jre6\bin\javaw.ex
Berkeley University                                                          ▲
Market Street
Polo Alto
Cuptino

                                                                            ▼
◄                                                                          ►
```

Mediator Pattern Case

Mediator Pattern : Defines simplified communication between classes. Define an object that encapsulates how a set of objects interact. Mediator promotes loose coupling by keeping objects from referring to each other explicitly, and it lets you vary their interaction independently.

1. Client wants to rent a house through an intermediary contact the HouseOwner

2. UML Diagram

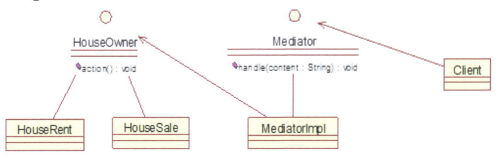

HouseOwner.java in **package com.mediator.cases;**

```java
public interface HouseOwner {

    public void action();
}
```

HouseRent.java in **package com.mediator.cases;**

```java
public class HouseRent implements HouseOwner {

    public void action() {
        System.out.println("Client come to rent a house");
    }
}
```

HouseSale.java in **package com.mediator.cases;**

```java
public class HouseSale implements HouseOwner {

    @Override
    public void action() {
        System.out.println("Client come to need to sell");
    }
}
```

Mediator.java in **package com.mediator.cases;**

```java
public interface Mediator {

    public void handle(String content);
}
```

MediatorImpl.java in **package com.mediator.cases;**

```java
public class MediatorImpl implements Mediator {
    private HouseOwner owner1;
    private HouseOwner owner2;

    public MediatorImpl() {
        owner1 = new HouseRent();
        owner2 = new HouseSale();
    }

    @Override
    public void handle(String content) {
        if ("rent".equals(content)) {
            owner1.action();
        }
        if ("sale".equals(content)) {
            owner2.action();
        }
    }
}
```

2. Create a Test class : TestMediator.java in package com.mediator.cases;

```java
public class TestMediator {
    public static void main(String[] args) {
        Mediator mediator = new MediatorImpl();

        //mediator help adjust the renting and selling between the client and the houseowner
        mediator.handle("rent");
        mediator.handle("sale");
    }
}
```

Result:

```
Problems  @ Javadoc  Declaration  Console ⊠

<terminated> TestMediator (1) [Java Application] C:\Program Files (x86)\Java\jre6\bin\javaw.e
Client come to rent a house
Client come to need to sell
```

Memento Pattern Case

Memento Pattern :
Capture the state of an object and save it. The object can be restored from original saved state in the future.

1. **Notepad++ Undo, redo, history recovery, etc.**

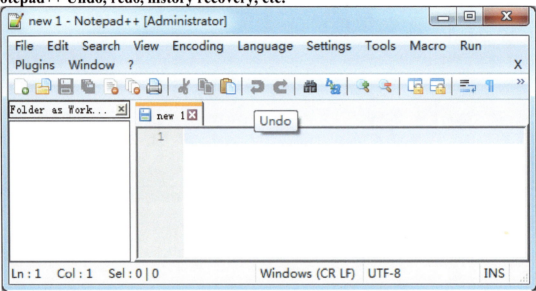

2. **UML Diagram**

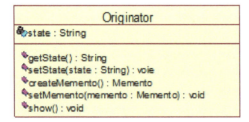

Memento.java in package com.memento.cases;

```java
public class Memento {
    private String state;

    public Memento(String state) {
        super();
        this.state = state;
    }

    public String getState() {
        return state;
    }

    public void setState(String state) {
        this.state = state;
    }
}
```

Notepad.java in package com.memento.cases;

```java
import java.util.Stack;

public class Notepad {
    private Stack<Memento> mementos;
    private int index;

    public Notepad() {
        mementos = new Stack<Memento>();
    }

    public void push(Memento memento) {
        mementos.push(memento);
        index++;
    }

    public Memento forward() {
        Memento memento = (Memento) mementos.get(index);
        index++;
        return memento;
    }

    public Memento back() {
        index--;
        Memento memento = (Memento) mementos.get(index);

        return memento;
    }
}
```

Originator.java in package com.memento.cases;

```java
public class Originator {
    private String state;

    public Originator() {
        super();
    }

    public String getState() {
        return state;
    }

    public void setState(String state) {
        this.state = state;
    }

    public Memento createMemento() {
        return new Memento(state);
    }

    public void setMemento(Memento memento) {
        this.state = memento.getState();
    }

    public void show() {
        System.out.println(state);
    }
}
```

2. Create a Test class : TestMemento.java in package com.memento.cases;

```java
public class TestMemento {

  public static void main(String[] args) {

    Notepad notepad = new Notepad();
    //Enter text in Notepad, save while saving
    Originator orig = new Originator();
    orig.setState("Move you in the direction of your dream.");
    notepad.push(orig.createMemento());

    orig.setState("Ways to start your day positively.");
    notepad.push(orig.createMemento());
    orig.setState("Love can change the world.");
    orig.show();

    //Undo redo   Recovery history
    orig.setMemento(notepad.back());
    orig.show();
    orig.setMemento(notepad.back());
    orig.show();

    System.out.println("----------------------------");

    orig.setMemento(notepad.forward());
    orig.show();
    orig.setMemento(notepad.forward());
    orig.show();
  }
}
```

Result:

```
Problems  @ Javadoc  Declaration  Console
Love can change the world.
Ways to start your day positively.
Move you in the direction of your dream.
----------------------------
Move you in the direction of your dream.
Ways to start your day positively.
```

Observer Pattern Principle

Observer Pattern : A way of notifying change to a number of classes. Define a one-to-many dependency between objects so that when one object changes state, all its dependents are notified and updated automatically.

1. In the stock market, stock data changes at any time. Sellers and buyers can see changes at any time.

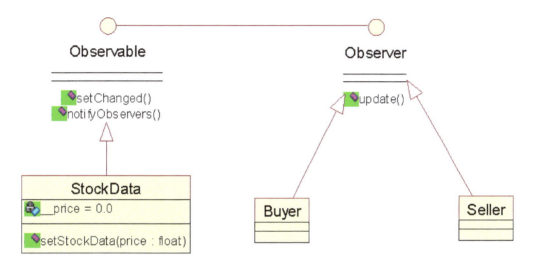

StockData.java in **package com.observer.principle;**

```java
import java.util.*;
public class StockData extends Observable {
   private float price;

   public StockData(float price) {
      super();
      this.price = price;
   }

   public float getPrice() {
      return price;
   }

   public void setPrice(float price) {
      this.price = price;
   }

   public void setStockData(float price) {
      this.price = price;
      setChanged();
      notifyObservers();
   }
}
```

Buyer.java in **package com.observer.principle;**

```java
import java.util.*;
public class Buyer implements Observer
{
   public Buyer(Observable o){
      o.addObserver(this);
   }

   public void update(Observable o, Object arg){
      if(o instanceof StockData){
         StockData data=(StockData)o;
         System.out.println("Buyer Price:"+data.getPrice());
      }
   }
}
```

Seller.java in package com.observer.principle;

```java
import java.util.Observable;
import java.util.Observer;

public class Seller implements Observer
{
    public Seller(Observable o)
    {
        o.addObserver(this);
    }

    public void update(Observable o, Object arg)
    {
        if(o instanceof StockData)
        {
            StockData data=(StockData)o;
            System.out.println("Seller Price:"+data.getPrice());
        }
    }

}
```

2. Create a Test class : TestObserver.java **in** package com.observer.principle;

```java
public class TestObserver {

    public static void main(String[] args) {
        StockData data = new StockData(16.9f);

        Buyer buyer = new Buyer(data);
        Seller seller = new Seller(data);

        data.setStockData(18.9f);

        System.out.println("-----------------------");

        data.setStockData(12.9f);
    }

}
```

Result:

```
Seller Price:18.9
Buyer Price:18.9
------------------------
Seller Price:12.9
Buyer Price:12.9
```

Observer Pattern Case

Observer Pattern :

producer and consumer models.

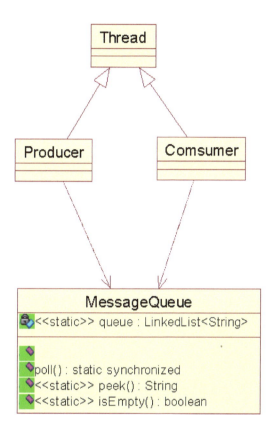

MessageQueue.java in package com.observer.cases;

```java
import java.util.LinkedList;

public class MessageQueue {

    private static LinkedList<String> queue = new LinkedList<String>();

    public static synchronized void push(String value) {

        queue.push(value);
    }

    public static synchronized String poll() {

        return queue.poll();
    }

    public static String peek(String value) {

        return queue.peek();
    }

    public static boolean isEmpty() {
        return queue.isEmpty();
    }

}
```

Producer.java in package com.observer.cases;

```java
public class Producer extends Thread {

    public void run() {
        for (int i = 0; i < 10; i++) {
            String message = "New Message : " + i;
            MessageQueue.push(message);
        }
    }
}
```

Comsumer.java in package com.observer.cases;

```java
public class Comsumer extends Thread {

    public static boolean isRun = true;

    @Override
    public void run() {
        while (isRun) {
            if (!MessageQueue.isEmpty()) {
                String message = MessageQueue.poll();
                System.out.println(message);
            }

            try {
                Thread.sleep(1000);
            } catch (InterruptedException e) {
                e.printStackTrace();
            }
        }
    }
}
```

2. Create a Test class : TestMessageQueue.java in package com.observer.cases;

```java
public class TestMessageQueue {

    public static void main(String[] args) {

        new Producer().start();//start producer thread

        new Comsumer().start();//start comsumer thread

    }

}
```

Result:

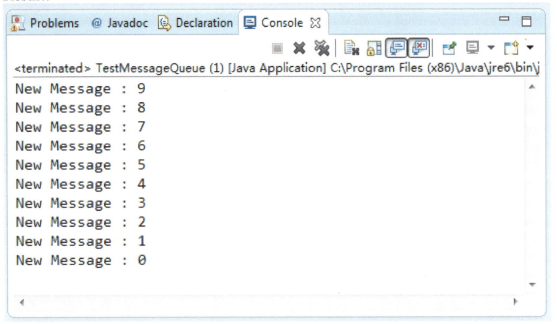

Visitor Pattern Case

Visitor Pattern : Defines a new operation to a class without change. Represent an operation to be performed on the elements of an object structure. Visitor lets you define a new operation without changing the classes of the elements on which it operates.

1. When a man succeeds, there is a great woman behind him.
When a woman succeeds, there is mostly a man behind her.
A man is in love
A woman is in love

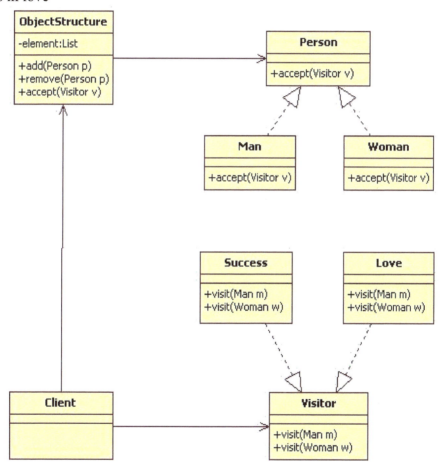

Person.java in package com.visitor.cases;

```java
public interface Person {

   void accept(Visitor visitor);

}
```

Man.java in package com.visitor.cases;

```java
public class Man implements Person {

   public void accept(Visitor visitor) {
      visitor.visit(this);
   }
}
```

Woman.java in package com.visitor.cases;

```java
public class Woman implements Person {

   public void accept(Visitor visitor) {
      visitor.visit(this);
   }
}
```

Visitor.java in package com.visitor.cases;

```java
public interface Visitor {

    public void visit(Man man);

    public void visit(Woman w);

}
```

Success.java in package com.visitor.cases;

```java
public class Success implements Visitor {

    public void visit(Man man) {
        System.out.println("When a man succeeds, there is a great woman behind him.");
    }

    public void visit(Woman girl) {
        System.out.println("When a woman succeeds, there is mostly a man behind her.");
    }
}
```

Love.java in package com.visitor.cases;

```java
public class Love implements Visitor {

    public void visit(Man man) {
        System.out.println("A man is in love");
    }

    public void visit(Woman girl) {
        System.out.println("A woman is in love");
    }

}
```

ObjectStructure.java in **package com.visitor.cases;**

```java
import java.util.*;

public class ObjectStructure {
    private List<Person> elements = new ArrayList<Person>();

    public void attach(Person element) {
        elements.add(element);
    }

    public void detach(Person element) {
        elements.remove(elements);
    }

    //Traverse various concrete elements and execute their accept methods
    public void display(Visitor visitor) {
        for (Person p : elements) {
            p.accept(visitor);
        }
    }
}
```

2. Create a Test class : TestVisitor.java in package com.visitor.cases;

```java
public class TestVisitor {

  public static void main(String[] args) {

    ObjectStructure o = new ObjectStructure();

    o.attach(new Man());
    o.attach(new Woman());

    Visitor success = new Success();
    o.display(success);

    Visitor amativeness = new Love();
    o.display(amativeness);

  }
}
```

Result:

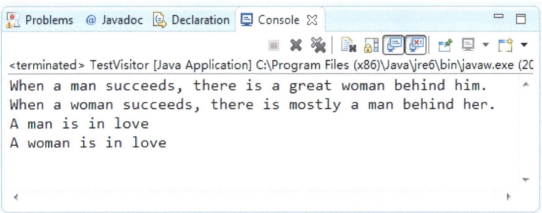

```
Problems  @ Javadoc  Declaration  Console ⊠

<terminated> TestVisitor [Java Application] C:\Program Files (x86)\Java\jre6\bin\javaw.exe (20
When a man succeeds, there is a great woman behind him.
When a woman succeeds, there is mostly a man behind her.
A man is in love
A woman is in love
```

State Pattern Case

State Pattern :

In a variety of states, a manager determines the different needs of the customer's needs in different states

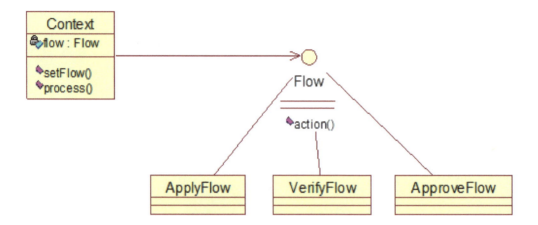

Flow.java in **package com.state.cases;**

```java
public interface Flow {

    public void action();
}
```

ApplyFlow.java in **package com.state.cases;**

```java
public class ApplyFlow implements Flow {

    @Override
    public void action() {
        System.out.println("Apply");
    }

}
```

VerfiyFlow.java in package com.state.cases;

```java
public class VerfiyFlow implements Flow {

    @Override
    public void action() {
        System.out.println("Verfiy");
    }

}
```

ApproveFlow.java in package com.state.cases;

```java
public class ApproveFlow implements Flow {

    @Override
    public void action() {
        System.out.println("Approve");
    }

}
```

Context.java in package com.state.cases;

```java
public class Context {
    private Flow flow;

    public void setFlow(Flow flow) {
        this.flow = flow;
    }

    public void process() {
        flow.action();
    }
}
```

2. Create a Test class : TestFlowState.java in package com.state.cases;

```java
public class TestFlowState {

    public static void main(String[] args) {
        Context ctx = new Context();
        ctx.setFlow(new ApplyFlow());
        ctx.process();

        ctx.setFlow(new VerfiyFlow());
        ctx.process();

        ctx.setFlow(new ApproveFlow());
        ctx.process();
    }

}
```

Result:

```
<terminated> TestFlowState [Java Application] C:\Program Files (x86)\Java\jre6\bin\javaw.exe
Apply
Verfiy
Approve
```

Proxy Pattern Principle

Proxy Pattern : An object representing another object. Provide a surrogate or placeholder for another object to control access to it.

1. Agency regist and study abroad

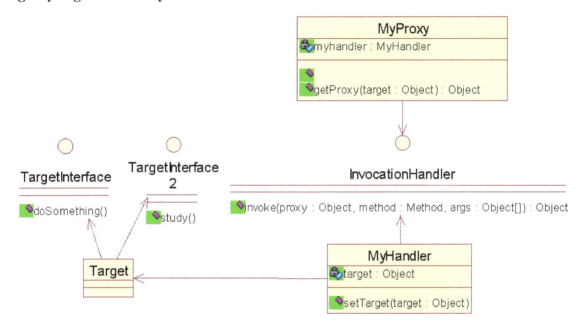

TargetInterface.java in package com.proxy.principle;

```java
public interface TargetInterface {

    public void doSomething();

}
```

TargetInterface2.java in package com.proxy.principle;

```java
public interface TargetInterface2 {

    public void study();

}
```

Target.java in package com.proxy.principle;

```java
public class Target implements TargetInterface, TargetInterface2 {

    @Override
    public void doSomething() {
        System.out.println("Agency registration company");
    }

    @Override
    public void study() {
        System.out.println("Agent for studying abroad");
    }
}
```

MyHandler.java in package com.proxy.principle;

```java
import java.lang.reflect.*;

public class MyHandler implements InvocationHandler {
    private Object target;

    public void setTarget(Object target) {
        this.target = target;
    }

    @Override
    public Object invoke(Object proxy, Method method, Object[] args) throws Throwable {
        System.out.println("before");
        method.invoke(target, args);
        System.out.println("after");
        return null;
    }

}
```

MyProxy.java in package com.proxy.principle;

```java
import java.lang.reflect.Proxy;

public class MyProxy {

    private MyHandler myhandler;

    public void setMyHandler(MyHandler myhandler) {
        this.myhandler = myhandler;
    }

    public Object getProxy(Object target) {
        //Agent help returns all possible interfaces that myhandler will handle
        return Proxy.newProxyInstance(MyProxy.class.getClassLoader(),
target.getClass().getInterfaces(), myhandler);
    }
}
```

2. Create a Test class : TestProxy.java in package com.proxy.principle;

```java
public class TestProxy {

  public static void main(String[] args) {

    Target target = new Target();
    //I am going to deal with the target
    MyHandler myhandler = new MyHandler();
    myhandler.setTarget(target);

    //Agent help handle the target
    MyProxy proxy = new MyProxy();
    proxy.setMyHandler(myhandler);

    TargetInterface targetInterface=(TargetInterface)proxy.getProxy(target);
    targetInterface.doSomething();

    System.out.println("--------------------------------------");

    TargetInterface2 targetInterface2= (TargetInterface2) proxy.getProxy(target);
    targetInterface2.study();

  }
}
```

Result:

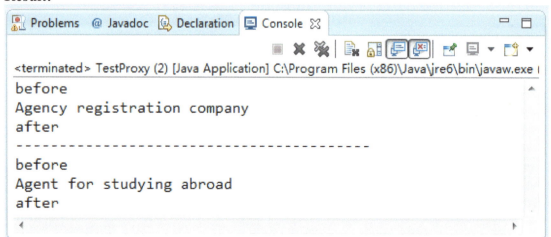

124

Proxy Pattern Case

Proxy Pattern :

Provide a proxy for other objects to control access to this object.

1. AOP aspect-oriented programming

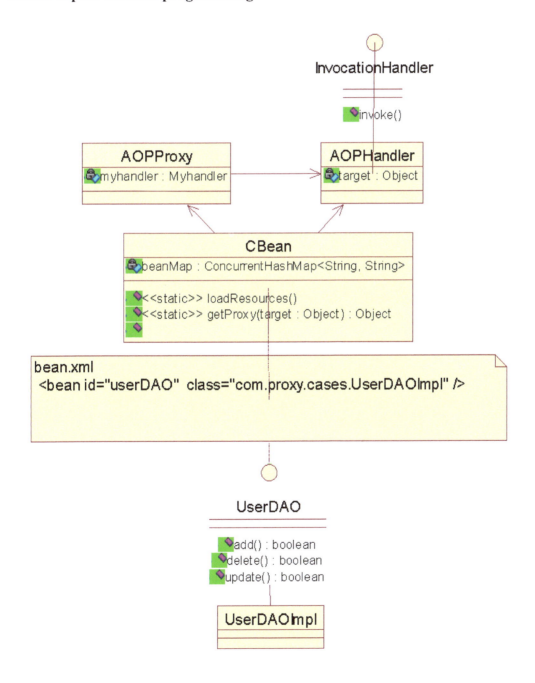

AOPHandler.java in

```java
import java.lang.reflect.*;

public class AOPHandler implements InvocationHandler {
    private Object target; //Facet object

    public void setTarget(Object target) {
        this.target = target;
    }

    @Override
    public Object invoke(Object proxy, Method method, Object[] args) throws Throwable {
        System.out.println("before");
        Object returnObj = method.invoke(target, args);
        System.out.println("after");
        return returnObj;
    }

}
```

AOPProxy.java in

```java
import java.lang.reflect.Proxy;

public class AOPProxy {

    private AOPHandler myhandler;

    public void setAOPHandler(AOPHandler myhandler) {
        this.myhandler = myhandler;
    }

    public Object getProxy(Object target) {
        return Proxy.newProxyInstance(AOPProxy.class.getClassLoader(),
target.getClass().getInterfaces(), myhandler);
    }
}
```

UserDAO.java in package com.proxy.cases;

```java
public interface UserDAO {

    public boolean add();

    public boolean delete();

    public boolean update();

}
```

UserDAOImpl.java in package com.proxy.cases;

```java
public class UserDAOImpl implements UserDAO {

    public UserDAOImpl() {

    }

    @Override
    public boolean add() {
        System.out.println("Add User");
        return false;
    }

    @Override
    public boolean delete() {
        System.out.println("Delete User");
        return false;
    }

    @Override
    public boolean update() {
        System.out.println("Update User");
        return false;
    }

}
```

Create **bean.xml** in **src**

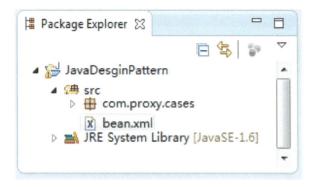

```xml
<?xml version="1.0" encoding="UTF-8"?>
<beans>
    <bean id="userDAO"  class="com.proxy.cases.UserDAOImpl" />
</beans>
```

Download the jar package for parsing XML
dom4j-1.6.1.jar
jaxen-1.1-beta-6.jar

http://en.verejava.com/download.jsp?id=1

add jar to Project
dom4j-1.6.1.jar , jaxen-1.1-beta-6.jar

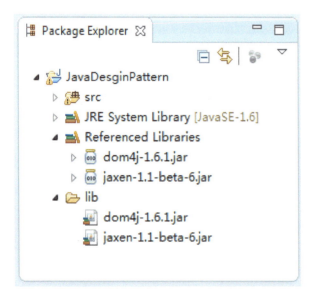

CBean.java in package com.proxy.cases;

```java
import java.io.*;
import java.util.List;
import java.util.concurrent.ConcurrentHashMap;
import org.dom4j.*;
public class CBean {
    private static ConcurrentHashMap<String, String> beanMap = new
ConcurrentHashMap<String, String>();

    static {
        loadResources();
    }

    public static void loadResources() {
        InputStream is = null;
        try {
            // SAXReader read
            SAXReader reader = new SAXReader();
            Object obj = new Object();
            String classAbsolutePath = obj.getClass().getResource("/").getPath() + "/bean.xml";
            String filePath = classAbsolutePath;
            is = new FileInputStream(filePath);

            if (is == null) {
                return;
            }
            Document doc = reader.read(is);
            List<Element> elementList = doc.selectNodes("/beans/bean");
            for (Element element : elementList) {
                String id = element.attributeValue("id");
                String clazz = element.attributeValue("class");
                beanMap.put(id, clazz);
            }
        } catch (Exception e) {
            e.printStackTrace();
        } finally {
            try {
                is.close();
            } catch (IOException e) {
                e.printStackTrace();
            }
        }
    }
}
```

```java
private static Object getProxy(Object target) {
    AOPHandler myhandler = new AOPHandler();
    myhandler.setTarget(target);
    AOPProxy proxy = new AOPProxy();
    proxy.setAOPHandler(myhandler);
    return proxy.getProxy(target);
}

public static Object getBean(String beanName) {
    String clazzName = beanMap.get(beanName);
    Class clazz = null;
    Object obj = null;
    try {
        clazz = Class.forName(clazzName);
        obj = clazz.newInstance();
    } catch (ClassNotFoundException e) {
        e.printStackTrace();
    } catch (InstantiationException e) {
        e.printStackTrace();
    } catch (IllegalAccessException e) {
        e.printStackTrace();
    }
    return getProxy(obj);
}
}
```

Result:

```
Problems  @ Javadoc  Declaration  Console ✕

before
Add User
after
-----------------------
before
Delete User
after
-----------------------
before
Update User
after
```

130

Thanks for learning

https://www.amazon.com/dp/B08HTXMXVY

https://www.amazon.com/dp/B08BWT6RCT

If you enjoyed this book and found some benefit in reading this, I'd like to hear from you and hope that you could take some time to post a review on Amazon. Your feedback and support will help us to greatly improve in future and make this book even better.

You can follow this link now.

http://www.amazon.com/review/create-review?&asin=109589935X

Different country reviews only need to modify the amazon domain name in the link:
www.amazon.co.uk
www.amazon.de
www.amazon.fr
www.amazon.es
www.amazon.it
www.amazon.ca
www.amazon.nl
www.amazon.in
www.amazon.co.jp
www.amazon.com.br
www.amazon.com.mx
www.amazon.com.au

I wish you all the best in your future success!

www.ingramcontent.com/pod-product-compliance
Lightning Source LLC
Chambersburg PA
CBHW041427050326
40689CB00003B/682